# WRITE WITH LIONS

# WRITE WITH LIONS

## WRITTEN BY:
## JIM MARKUS

## ILLUSTRATED BY:
## NICOLE MEEKHOF

2013
Book by Jim Markus
Illustrations by Nicole Meekhof in 2013
Printed in the United States
MoreKnown Books and Daydream Alchemy Press


ISBN: 978-0-9894106-0-1

# FOR STORYTELLERS

# CONTENTS

**Illustrated Fables**

# INTRODUCTION

Fables are succinct little stories that espouse morals. Personified animals argue with each other. They hunt prey. They learn lessons.

A fable's simplicity allows it to be told and retold. Generation after generation, we share fables. Some become mirrors of the societies where they were born. The most famous fables are attributed to Aesop, an idealized Greek fabulist, a composer of fables, who might never have existed at all. Even now, he is credited with work that never existed in his time.

If Aesop did exist, none of his original writings survive today. The philosopher Aristotle says Aesop was born as a slave in 620 BCE. However, the *Aesop Romance*, a fictionalized account of his life, tells of Aesop's remarkable rise in social standing through the use of his clever wit. The fables that we have today were likely written by contemporaries. Their primary use would have been as collections for orators.

The oral tradition of storytelling extends far beyond Europe and long before Aesop. Short stories that feature animals as protagonists are celebrated across the world. The famous trickster spider, Anansi, sometimes known as the god of all stories, was born in African stories. Vali is a famous monkey king that survives in Indian traditions. Anansi and Vali both moralize in their stories, leaving readers to contemplate the deeper meaning in their words.

Some notable modern characters come from tropes found in old fables. Even today, trickster foxes appear in modern cartoons. We warn against the wolf in sheep's clothing. Lions were crowned in

Aesop's world long before film companies animated them. Some of the most well recognized movies and television shows were inspired by characters in these stories.

Modern fables can be found everywhere. That is what *Write with Lions* is all about. We are here to tell stories that have been told before. We will tell them in new ways, sometimes with new characters, sometimes with the help of classic tropes. The fables inside are included to help convey the idea of the original story. The prompts and games allow us to create something totally new.

Fables are ideal writing companions. Their archetypical characters lack detailed personalities and offer room for creative expansion. Their simple plots preach morals and, because they appeal to such wide audiences, most settings can be altered or omitted without impacting the story.

Use this book as a well. Come when you are thirsty for inspiration. Drink until you are sated.

# USING THIS BOOK

Now that you have your own copy of *Write with Lions*, you might be wondering about the best way to use it. We created these suggestions not as an ordered list, but as three simple suggestions to approach the fables, exercises, and games inside. Some storytellers find inspiration in restrictions. Others create their best stories without too much structure. Might we suggest that you . . .

**1. Read it in order.**

If you are looking to experiment with your writing, to practice your craft, and to challenge yourself with a formal challenge, follow the structure of this book in order. Read the first fable. Complete each prompt for that fable. Read the next fable. Complete each of the next prompts. Continue. At the end, you will complete well over 200 pieces of writing. Once you finish, read and revise your work. Experiment with your stories. Learn from them. Submit them to contests and journals.

**2. Haphazardly explore.**

If you are looking to break through writer's block or are having difficulty getting started for the day, flip the book open to a random fable and start writing. You'll find inspiration in every one of these fables. Every fable has a few writing prompts to drive you in a specific direction. Use the bits and pieces to launch your writing and don't stop until you finish.

## 3. Write from the illustrations.

Nicole is a supremely talented artist. She illustrated the print copy of this book so we could draw inspiration from images as well as fables. Choose an illustration. Use it as a writing exercise. Deviate from the fable. Create something new.

# FABLES

# THE KINGDOM OF THE LION

All of the animals of the field and forest had a lion as their king. He was neither cruel, nor tyrannical, but just as gentle as a king could be. During his reign he made a royal proclamation for a general assembly of all the birds and beasts, and drew up conditions for a universal league, in which the wolf and the lamb, the panther and the kid, the tiger and the stag, the dog and the hare, should live together in perfect peace and amity.

The hare said, "Finally, the weak shall take their place with impunity by the side of the strong!" After the hare said this, he ran for his life.

# AESOP'S TIP

*Speak honestly but be prepared for harsh responses to your work. The Hare left his words to their own merit. Writers are wise to do the same.*

# WRITING PROMPTS

I.   Describe an event from earlier in the hare's life where he learned to mistrust the stronger animals of the forest.

II.  Write about the lion's ascent to royalty. Why does he lead the beasts of the field and the forest?

III. Write about this royal proclamation from the point of view of one of the wolves or panthers.

IV.  Write a new proclamation from the lion.

V.   How would this fable have been written in the style of your favorite genre? Consider rewriting this as a romance, science fiction, or mystery.

# THE MISER

A miser sold all that he had and bought a lump of gold, which he buried in a hole in the ground by the side of an old wall, and went to look at daily. One of his workmen noticed his frequent visits to the spot and decided to watch his movements. He soon discovered the secret of the hidden treasure and, digging down, came to the lump of gold and stole it.

The miser, on his next visit, found the hole empty and began to tear his hair and to make loud lamentations.

A neighbor, seeing him overcome with grief and learning the cause, said, "Don't fret; go and take a stone and place it in the hole. Imagine that the gold is still lying there. It will do you quite the same service; for when the gold was there, you had it not, as you did not make the slightest use of it."

# AESOP'S TIP

*Do not store your passion for writing under a rock in the corner of your garden. The more you use it, the more it grows. The world is filled with writers who hide their talents, afraid of bringing anything into the world. The more you write, the better your writing.*

# WRITING PROMPTS

I. Assume the miser has a criminal past. Write about how he came upon his great fortune before he sold it all to buy the lump of gold.

II. Consider that the miser's neighbor was the same workman who stole the gold. Give him a reason for having done so.

III. How would Sir Arthur Conan Doyle, author of the famed Sherlock Holmes mysteries, have written this story? Write *The Miser* as a detective story. Consider using the characters from Doyle's stories as inspiration.

IV. What would the neighbor have done with the same amount of gold? Tell his story as if he were a man of equal wealth to the miser.

V. Write a conversation between two of the miser's workmen.

VI. Write a letter from the miser to his workmen. Consider writing the letter from a time before his gold was stolen.

# THE FOX AND THE GOAT

A fox one day fell into a deep well and could find no means of escape. A goat, overcome with thirst, came to the same well, and seeing the fox, inquired if the water was good.

Concealing his sad plight under a merry guise, the fox praised the water, saying it was excellent beyond measure, and encouraging him to descend. The goat, mindful only of his thirst, thoughtlessly jumped down, but just as he drank, the fox informed him of the difficulty they were both in and suggested a scheme for their common escape.

The fox replied, "If you will place your forefeet upon the wall and bend your head, I will run up your back and escape, and will help you out afterward." The goat readily assented and the fox leaped upon his back. Steadying himself with the goat's horns, he safely reached the mouth of the well and made off as fast as he could.

When the goat cried out at him for breaking his promise, the fox turned around and cried out, "You fool! If you had as many brains in your head as you have hairs in your beard, you would never have gone down before you had inspected the way up, nor would you have exposed yourself to dangers from which you had no means of escape."

# AESOP'S TIP

*Look before you leap. Before accepting a writing assignment, make sure to understand the expectations and the audience. Don't be afraid to ask questions.*

# WRITING PROMPTS

I. This fable has appeared in many forms since Aesop's time. Use the scheme of "trapped trickster traps foolish helper" in a modern tale.

II. Write the fable from the point of view of either character.

III. Write an alternate ending to the fable where the goat escapes the well. Decide whether the goat seeks out the fox again.

IV. Rewrite this fable using new characters in a city. They might find themselves trapped in a sewer, on the roof of a building, or in a locked room.

V. How did the fox fall into the well? Describe where he came from and where he was going.

# THE MAN AND THE LION

A man and a lion traveled together through the forest. As they hiked, each boasted of his superiority in strength and prowess.

As they were arguing, they passed a statue carved in stone, which represented a lion being strangled by a man. The traveler pointed to it and said, "See how strong we are? We prevail over even the king of beasts."

The lion replied, "This statue was made by one of you men. If we lions knew how to erect statues, you would see the man placed under the paw of the lion."

# AESOP'S TIP

*A good writer understands the objective truths in a story; a great writer uses subjective viewpoints to better describe her characters.*

*Where one person sees victory, another sees betrayal. Where one person sees chaos, another sees opportunity. As you explore a story, consider the viewpoints of several characters.*

*Everyone tells her own story.*

# WRITING PROMPTS

I.   Tell the lion's story. Imagine that they encountered a statue of a man under the paw of a lion.

II.  Tell the story of the statue, the one of the man strangling a lion. What led to this monstrous end?

III. How did the lion and the man in the fable meet? Why are they traveling together?

IV.  Rewrite the fable using current celebrities or political figures.

V.   Perhaps the statue was created as a warning to lions in the forest. Describe who built it and why it was neccesary at the time.

VI.  Write a legend for the lions. Tell the story of one of the greatest lions of the forest.

# THE FLIES AND THE HONEY-POT

A number of flies were attracted to a jar of honey that had been overturned in a housekeeper's room. When they placed their feet in it, they ate greedily. Their feet, however, became so smeared with the honey that they could not use their wings. Unable to escape, they were suffocated. Just as the flies were expiring, they exclaimed, "We are such foolish creatures, for the sake of a little pleasure we have destroyed ourselves."

# AESOP'S TIP

*Pleasure, bought with pain, hurts. There is no magic serum that makes better writers. Be wary of anyone who says otherwise. Writers often seek to justify addiction, saying that other addicts achieved fame and wealth. Many forget that these people gained notoriety in spite of their shortcomings, not because of them.*

# WRITING PROMPTS

I.   Create a modern story using the same moral.

II.  Reimagine this story in a science fiction world. One group of individuals in this world stumbles onto an overturned truck that has crashed on the side of a road. What was in the truck? How did it affect everyone in the group?

III. Write a story where pleasure bought with pain ends with a positive outcome.

IV.  Tell the story of the first fly to find the overturned pot of honey.

V.   Write a diabolical plan that a mad scientist might use to take over the world using the lesson learned from the overturned honeypot.

# THE ANTS AND THE GRASSHOPPER

The ants were spending a fine winter's day drying grain collected in the summertime. A grasshopper, perishing with famine, passed by and earnestly begged for a little food.

The ants inquired of him, "Why did you not treasure up food during the summer?"

He replied, "I had not leisure enough. I passed the days in singing."

The ants answered, "If you were foolish enough to sing all summer, you must dance hungry to bed in winter."

# AESOP'S TIP

*It is best to work like an ant during the times when you can be productive. Only those who are prepared are able to seize new opportunities.*

*Build your repertoire by writing even when everyone else is singing with the grasshoppers.*

# WRITING PROMPTS

I. Write this story from the point of view of the grasshopper, a well-respected artist who sang during the summer months.

II. Write this story from the point of view of the ants, who worked without rest during the summer months.

III. This story is one of the most well known of Aesop's fables and comes up often as a lesson in financial independence. Write a letter from the grasshopper to his son after being turned away by the ants.

IV. Write a letter from one ant to another, describing her winter holiday.

V. The ants stored their food in preparation. The grasshopper sang during the summer and suffered through the cold months. What other strategies did animals of the forest use to prepare for the winter?

# HERCULES AND THE WAGONER

A carter was driving a wagon along a country lane, when the wheels sank down deep into a rut. The rustic driver, stupefied and aghast, stood looking at the wagon and cried loudly to Hercules to come and help him.

Hercules, it is said, appeared and said, "Put your shoulders to the wheels, my man. Start goading your oxen. Never more pray to me for help until you have done your best to help yourself, or depend upon it you will henceforth pray in vain."

# AESOP'S TIP

*Self help is the best kind of help. Edit your writing before asking anyone else to read it. Be your own critic first. Write freely, then critique hard. Use several drafts. Be resourceful. Only after the piece is ready should you seek help.*

# WRITING PROMPTS

I.  Why did the carter cry out for help before attempting anything himself? Write a letter from the carter to Hercules apologizing for his intrusion and justifying his actions.

II.  Hercules was in the middle of an important contest when he heard the cries of the carter. Tell the story of the contest and why Hercules was upset to be dragged away from it.

III.  Rewrite this fable using other deities. Focus on their differing responses to the same situation. What morals might they share with the carter?

IV.  As Hercules, write a chapter from a self-help book for carters.

V.  Tell the story of why the road was so muddy that the cart's wheels sank into the muck.

VI.  Assume the carter was on his way to bring supplies home from the market. Write about the family as they waited for his return. What did the family expect to be delivered?

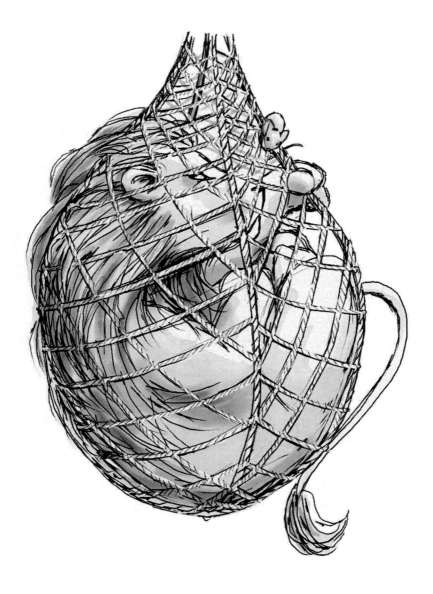

# THE LION AND THE
# MOUSE

A lion was awakened from sleep by a mouse running over his face. Rising up angrily, he caught her and was about to kill her, when the mouse begged, "If you would only spare my life, I would be sure to repay your kindness." The lion laughed and let her go.

It happened shortly after this that the lion was caught by some hunters, who bound him by strong ropes in a net. The mouse, recognizing his roar, came and gnawed the rope with her teeth, and set him free.

"You ridiculed the idea," the mouse said, "of my ever being able to help you, not expecting to receive from me any repayment of your favor; now you know that it's possible for such a small mouse to help the mightiest of beasts."

# AESOP'S TIP

*Be generous with your words. Even when you think you have the least to gain, find time to use your talent in a way that helps others. Sometimes it's best to let the mouse live.*

# WRITING PROMPTS

I. Write a fable using the hunters who captured the lion with strong ropes. What lessons did they learn?

II. Describe what happened with the other members of the lion's pride when they found out he let a mouse escape.

III. Write a journal entry from the mouse from the night she was spared by the lion. Consider that her meeting with the lion was not the most surprising thing to happen to her that day.

IV. The fable does not show much of the ridicule that the mouse mentioned. Rewrite the fable to include more detail. What else did the lion do or say that made the mouse feel ridiculed?

V. Write the same story using wealth and destitution to separate the two parties.

# THE CAT AND VENUS

A cat fell in love with a handsome young man and prayed that Venus change her into the form of a woman.

Venus consented to her request and transformed the cat into a beautiful damsel, so that the young man saw her and loved her, and took her home as his bride.

That same night, Venus, curious to discover if the cat in her change of shape had also altered her habits of life, let down a mouse in the middle of the room. The cat, quite forgetting her present condition, lept from the couch and pursued the mouse, wishing to eat it.

Venus was much disappointed and caused her to return to her former shape.

# AESOP'S TIP

*No matter the genre, your voice will show through. Great writers practice many styles and find success when they develop their own. Write and act as you wish to be known. Venus treats cats like cats.*

# WRITING PROMPTS

I. In this fable, a cat falls in love with a handsome young man. Describe how she fell in love. Where did she first see him? Who was he?

II. Venus transforms the cat into a beautiful damsel. What made this goddess take interest in a cat? Write about the importance of this specific cat and why she might merit divine attention.

III. At the end of the fable, the cat returns to her former shape. By this time, the handsome young man is already in love. How does he react? Consider allowing him to entreat another god for a favor.

IV. Write this as a myth involving another god. How would Artemis have interacted with these characters? Zeus?

V. What happened to the mouse? How was this mouse chosen to be the bait for Venus' trap?

# JUPITER AND THE MONKEY

Jupiter issued a proclamation to all the beasts of the forest and promised a royal reward to the one whose offspring should be deemed the handsomest.

A monkey came with the rest and presented, with all a mother's tenderness, a flat-nosed, hairless, ill-featured young monkey as a candidate for the promised reward. A general laugh saluted her on the presentation of her son.

She resolutely said, "I know not whether Jupiter will allot the prize to my son, but this I do know, that he is, at least in the eyes of his mother, the dearest, handsomest, and most beautiful of all."

# AESOP'S TIP

*Your stories will be dear to you. Remember that the rest of the world may not see the same beauty that you see. If you are not finding success with others, keep working. You might yet create something that earns the prize.*

# WRITING PROMPTS

I. In this fable, Jupiter reigns over the beasts of the forest. Why does he have this honor? Create an event in his history that explains why the animals follow him.

II. Describe the monkey's position in this forest. Aside from her pride in her son, what other traits define her? How do the animals treat her in daily life?

III. The monkey's son will eventually go on to do great or terrible things. What does he do with his life? Write about the monkey's son five years after this contest takes place.

IV. Write about another animal's entrance into the same contest. Who entered their son? How did this other family fare?

V. Be a journalist covering this monumentous event. Write an article about the contest.

VI. Jupiter chose three animals to act as judges. Write about each of them. Who did each want to win? Was it fair or biased?

# THE PIGLET, THE SHEEP, AND THE GOAT

A young pig was shut up in a fold-yard with a goat and a sheep. On one occasion when the shepherd grabbed hold of him, the little pig grunted and squeaked and resisted violently.

The sheep and the goat complained of his distressing cries, saying, "He often handles us, and we do not cry out."

The pig replied, "Your handling and mine are very different things. He only wants your wool or your milk, but he grabs at me for my very life."

# AESOP'S TIP

*Is your story a pig, a sheep, or a goat? Every story requires different handling. Slaughter some of your work. Shear others.*

# WRITING PROMPTS

I. The sheep and the goat complain about everything. They complain about the heat on sunny days. They complain about the quantity of feed during their morning meal. Write a conversation between the sheep and the goat after seeing the young pig carried away.

II. The young pig might have later been given to the shepherd's daughter as a pet. Write about another potential outcome for the young pig after being caught by the shepherd.

III. When the shepherd returned to milk the goat, he was kicked by all of the animals. Write about an uprising that might have occurred after the little pig disappeared.

IV. Write a story using the piglet, the sheep, and the goat fable as an ending.

V. Write the same fable from the point of view of the shepherd.

# THE MICE AND THE WEASELS

The weasels and the mice waged a perpetual war with each other, in which much blood was shed. The weasels were always the victors. The mice thought that the cause of their frequent defeats was that they had no specific leaders to command them and that they were exposed to danger from lack of discipline. They therefore chose as leaders mice that were most renowned for their family descent, strength, and counsel, as well as those most noted for their courage in the fight, so that they might be better train their soldiers and form a winning strategy.

When all this was done, and the army disciplined, and the herald mouse had proclaimed war by challenging the weasels, the newly chosen generals bound their heads with straws, so they might be more easily seen by all their troops.

Scarcely had the battle begun, when a great swarm of weasels overwhelmed the mice, who scampered off as fast as they could to their holes. The generals, not being able to get in on account of the ornaments on their heads, were all captured and eaten by the weasels.

# AESOP'S TIP

*Take pride in awards, but do not rest on your laurels. The generals who bound their heads in straw were too burdened to re-enter their homes and were easily captured by the weasels. A large ego draws the same burden.*

# WRITING PROMPTS

I.  Write about the first town hall meeting of the mice, where it was decided that the best among them might become generals.

II.  Write a letter from one of the generals to her family. Describe her life as she trained the army, before the herald mouse proclaimed the start of the war.

III.  Write about the massacre from the point of view of the herald mouse. He trumpeted the start of the war and was the first back in his hole shortly after.

IV.  Write an article for the Weasel World News describing the short battle.

V.  Rewrite the fable using a supernatural setting. Incorporate magic, monsters, or mythology.

# THE ONE-EYED DOE

A doe, blind in one eye, grazed as near to the edge of the cliff as she possibly could, seeking to secure her greater safety. She turned her sound eye towards the land so that she might quickly spot the approach of hunter or hound, and her injured eye towards the sea, where she entertained no anticipation of danger.

Some boatmen sailing by saw her and, seeing an unmoving target, shot an arrow into her side. In her last breath, she cried, "What a wretched creature I am! I guarded myself well against the land and was snared by the perils of the sea!"

# AESOP'S TIP

*Write for the land and the sea. Write for the sun, the moon, the living, the dead, the light, and the dark. When you write, think big.*

# WRITING PROMPTS

I. Describe the boatmen's journey. How long were they at sea before seeing the unsuspecting doe?

II. How long had the doe been coming to the edge of the cliff to graze? Describe how she found this spot and the dangers of the other locations that she had scouted.

III. Tell the story of how the doe lost her eye.

IV. Describe a day in the life of the boat captain. Write this in the form of a journal entry.

V. Tell the story of the boat captain's daughter.

VI. The doe had an older brother who survived to an old age. Tell about his encounters with this same cliff.

# THE WOLF AND THE SHEEP

A wolf, sorely wounded and bitten by dogs, lay sick and maimed in his lair. Hungry and thirsty, he called to a sheep who was passing and asked him to fetch some water from a stream that flowed close beside him. "If you will bring me drink," he said, "I will find means to provide myself with meat."

"Yes," said the sheep, "if I should bring you the water, you would doubtless make me provide the meat as well."

# AESOP'S TIP

*Write with honesty. Your audience will smell deceit just like the sheep did.*

# WRITING PROMPTS

I.  How did the wolf find himself surrounded by vicious dogs? Why did they attack him?

II. Where was the sheep going when he came across the wolf? Tell his story.

III. Explain how the wolf eventually finds water. Does the wolf survive?

IV. Rewrite the fable where the sheep is the mastermind behind the dogs' attack.

V.  Write a letter from the wolf to the sheep, a year before this famous exchange.

VI. Write this as a story from the point of view of the wolf.

# THE FOX AND THE CROW

A crow, having stolen a bit of meat, perched in a tree and held it in her beak. A fox saw her there and wanted the meat for himself.

"How handsome is the crow," he exclaimed, "in the beauty of her feathers and the grace of her flight. If her voice were only equal to her beauty, she would deservedly be considered the queen of birds!"

This he said deceitfully, but the crow, anxious to refute the statement, cawed loudly and dropped the flesh. The fox quickly picked it up and said, "My good crow, your voice is right enough, but your wit is wanting."

# AESOP'S TIP

*Accept criticism gracefully. Not everyone will like everything that you create. Accept honest critiques. Strive for improvement. Your work will sing on its own.*

# WRITING PROMPTS

I. The fox is a notorious trickster who makes many appearances in fables. Write about another of his tricks. Alternately, use the hare, the spider, or another trickster of your choosing.

II. Describe how the crow stole the bit of meat. Where did it come from?

III. Write about how the fox learned such wit earlier in the summer. Did it come from repartee with another animal or did he learn it from an instructor? Has he ever fallen victim to a similar trick?

IV. Write another story using the crow as the main character.

V. Write this as a story from the point of view of an outside observer. Consider using a hunter, a child, or a hermit who lives in the woods.

# THE BAT AND THE WEASELS

A bat, having fallen to the ground, was captured by a weasel and pleaded for his life. The weasel refused, saying that he was, by nature, the enemy of all birds. The bat assured him that he was not a bird, but a mouse, and thus was set free.

Shortly afterward the bat again fell to the ground and was caught by another weasel, whom he likewise entreated not to eat him. The weasel said that he had a special hostility to mice. The bat assured him that he was not a mouse, but a bat, and thus a second time escaped.

# AESOP'S TIP

*It is wise to consider your audience when crafting a story. Write as a mouse if the reader hates birds. Write as a bird when if the reader hates mice.*

# WRITING PROMPTS

I. Why did the bat keep falling to the ground? Write about why this bat found himself constantly falling out of the sky.

II. The two weasels later realized they had caught and released the same creature. What did they say? What did they conclude would be the right course of action should either of them come upon the bat again?

III. Why would the second weasel have a special hostility toward mice? Write about his last encounter with a mouse.

IV. Rewrite this fable without using the words bat, weasel, or mouse.

V. Tell another story using this same bat. Avoid the inclusion of weasels.

VI. Write this as an epistolary from the points of view of the bat and the weasels.

# THE WEASEL AND THE MICE

A weasel, inactive from age, was not able to catch mice as he once did. He therefore rolled himself in flour and lay down in a dark corner.

A mouse, supposing him to be food, leaped upon him, and was instantly caught and squeezed to death. Another perished in a similar manner, and then a third, and still others after them.

A very old mouse, who had escaped many traps during his youth, observed from a safe distance the trick of his crafty foe and said, "Weasel, I wish you success equal to your honesty."

# AESOP'S TIP

*The most effective arguments are those wrapped in flour and laying in dark corners. They do not actively seek converts. They surround themselves with agreeable odors. Only after the reader has digested it does the argument become apparent.*

# WRITING PROMPTS

I.  Write the fable from the point of view of the old mouse. Describe how he saw the weasel arrive and why he allowed so many other mice to die in this petard.

II.  The old mouse had escaped from many traps during his life. Describe the best trap that he was able to elude.

III.  How did the weasel respond to the old mouse's curse?

IV.  Write about one of the weasel's adventures from when he was young. Consider writing as a journal entry or news article.

V.  Rewrite the fable in the style of a science fiction drama.

VI.  Write a letter from the very old mouse to one of his favorite grandchildren.

# THE BOY SWIMMING

A boy, who had been swimming in a river, was in danger of being drowned. He called out to a passing traveler for help, but instead of holding out a helping hand, the man stood by and scolded the boy for his imprudence.

"Please," cried the boy, "help me now and scold me afterward."

# AESOP'S TIP

*Council without help is worthless.*

*When you critique the work of another writer, offer specific feedback. Describe what works. Offer concrete suggestions for improvement in areas that need work.*

# WRITING PROMPTS

I. Write about the man. What does he do for a living? Why would his first thought be to scold a drowning child?

II. Write about what happened after this fable ends. Does the boy survive or does the man let him drown? What are the implications for the man?

III. Write about another useless council. Consider using current events in your writing.

IV. Write another story using the man from this fable.

V. The fable does not mention the details of the boy's situation. Elaborate on how and why the boy is in danger of being drowned.

VI. Write this as a short story from the point of view of the passing traveler.

# THE FLEA AND THE MAN

A man, very much annoyed with a flea, caught him at last and said, "Who are you who dare to feed on my limbs and to cost me so much trouble in catching you?"

The flea replied, "My dear sir, please spare my life for I cannot possibly do you much harm."

The man, laughing, replied, "Now you shall certainly die by my hand. No evil, small or large, should ever be tolerated."

# AESOP'S TIP

*Fleas feed on humans. Humans kill fleas. Actions have consequences. Such is the case with the characters in your stories. Creat situations with serious consequences. Build dangerous worlds.*

# WRITING PROMPTS

I.   In its current form, the moral of the fable rests on its last line. Create a new story using the same characters. As a challenge, give it a different moral from the one Aesop chose. Consider the flea first as Aesop intended, a creature of evil. Then, consider the flea as the inverse, a noble creature.

II.   Write a short story about a man who did not see fleas as evil. In this story, the man should first let this small creature live. Either focus on the valor of his choice or the charisma of the flea.

III.   Rewrite this fable in the same style as the original. This time, give the flea a different plea. Decide whether it sways the man's decision or results in more conflict.

IV.   Write a formal plea for absolution on behalf of the flea. Consider writing as a figure of authority.

V.   What does the man do as a profession? Write about a day in the life of the man who was plagued with fleas.

# THE MISCHIEVOUS DOG

A dog used to run up quietly to the heels of everyone he met, and to bite them without notice. His master suspended a bell about his neck so that the dog might give notice of his presence wherever he went.

Thinking it a mark of distinction, the dog grew proud of his bell and went tinkling it all over the marketplace. One day an old hound said to him, "Why do you make such an exhibition of yourself? That bell that you carry is not, believe me, any order of merit. On the contrary, it is a mark of disgrace, a public notice to all men to avoid you as an ill-mannered dog."

# AESOP'S TIP

*Write flawed characters. Sometimes mischievous dogs see their bells as awards. Nobody understands the world objectively. As you develop your story, use this to your advantage.*

# WRITING PROMPTS

I.   Write about the dog's reaction to the old hound's news. What does he do when he returns home to his master?

II.   Why does the mischievous dog behave this way?

III.   The man who suspended the bell around the dog's neck has his own story. Describe the way that he originally met the dog.

IV.   Explain why the old hound reveals the importance of the bell to the dog. Connect the old hound to the dog's master in some way.

V.   Write a character description of someone with the same mistaken view of his own notoriety. Consider creating a minor, modern celebrity status for your character. How does he interact with others? Does anyone correct him?

# THE SICK STAG

A sick stag lay down in a quiet corner of its pasture-ground. His companions came in great numbers to inquire after his health. Each of these visitors took a share of the stag's food. Because of these greedy companions, the sick stag died, not from his sickness, but from the failure of the means of living.

# AESOP'S TIP

*Surround yourself with those you admire. Work with them. Play with them. Write with them. While evil companions bring more hurt than profit, good companions bring more profit than hurt.*

# WRITING PROMPTS

I.   The sick stag once served as companion to a great king. His illness occurred at the same time as the king's death. Write about how the stag came to know royalty. Include some of the stag's other companions in your story.

II.  Write about the detective who discovered that the stag had died from starvation. This detective uncovered a diabolical plot. Why was the stag killed? Were all of his companions culpable or was it a specific rival?

III. The stag was known to many on the farmlands where he lived. Write an article about why he might have been so famous.

IV.  Write a story using the sick stag fable as your ending.

V.   Write a short story from the point of view of an evil companion.

# THE WOLF IN SHEEP'S CLOTHING

Once upon a time a wolf resolved to disguise his appearance in order to secure food more easily. Encased in the skin of a sheep, he pastured with the flock, deceiving the shepherd by his costume.

In the evening he was shut up by the shepherd in the fold; the gate was closed, and the entrance made thoroughly secure. But the shepherd, returning to the fold during the night to obtain meat for the next day, mistakenly caught up the wolf instead of a sheep and killed him instantly.

# AESOP'S TIP

*Work in surprises for your characters. Surprise your shepherd; let the wolves in. Surprise your wolves; let the shepherd win.*

# WRITING PROMPTS

I.   Write this tale from the point of view of the shepherd after he has figured out what has happened.

II.   Write this tale from the point of view of one of the terrified sheep during the night preceding the wolf's death.

III.   Write this tale from the point of view of the wolf as he comes up with the idea for his disguise.

IV.   Rewrite the ending to this tale so that the wolf is discovered by the sheep during the night.

V.   Write about another disguise that the wolf had used before he came to this farm dressed as a sheep.

VI.   Many modern stories use the phrase "a wolf in sheep's clothing," but omit the moral "harm seek, harm find." Write another story where the antagonist, seeking to harm others, finds harm herself instead.

# THE BOASTING TRAVELER

A man who had traveled far and wide was boasting of the many wonderful and heroic feats he had performed in the different places he had visited. Among other things, he said that when he was at Rhodes he had leaped farther than any man. He said that there were many people who saw him do it and whom he could call as witnesses.

One of the bystanders interrupted him, saying, "If what you say is true, there is no need of witnesses. Suppose this be Rhodes and leap for us now."

# AESOP'S TIP

*Talk is cheap. Many dream of writing a book; few actually write. Suppose this be Rhodes and write your story.*

# WRITING PROMPTS

I.  While the moral of this fable might be obvious, write a story where the boasting traveler spoke the truth. Allow him to accept the challenge and take the leap.

II. After figuring out that the man was lying, how did his audience respond?

III. Tell the story of the jealous bystander who demanded proof of the traveler's claim.

IV. Write about other tall tales that the boasting traveler told to his friends upon his return.

V.  Describe the way that the boasting traveler's stories might have been elaborated, extended, and embellished by others who heard his words. What might he have said originally upon his return? What did that story turn into after being re-told by many people?

# THE HORSE AND GROOM

A groom used to spend whole days in currycombing and rubbing down his horse, but at the same time stole his oats and sold them for his own profit.

"Please!" said the horse. "If you really wish me to be in good condition, you should groom me less and feed me more."

# AESOP'S TIP

*Writers learn by writing. While editing is important, do not be distracted. Feed your work before you worry about grooming it.*

# WRITING PROMPTS

I.  Assuming that the horse cannot speak, write about the man learning the same lesson in a less direct way.

II. The groomer was paid by the horse's owner for the task of grooming. When he stole the oats and sold them for profit, he started living more comfortably. Give the man a reason for stealing the oats.

III. Tell the story of the horse's owner. How did she find the horse? How did she come to own it? Focus on the conflict in her own story.

IV. Describe why it is important that the horse be well groomed. Write a letter from the horse's owner to the groomer describing its importance.

V.  Describe how oats might work as a currency for horses in the stable. Create a society in the stable where the well groomed horse lives.

# THE GOAT AND THE GOATHERD

A goatherd had sought to bring back a stray goat to his flock. He whistled and sounded his horn in vain but the straggler paid no attention to the summons. At last the goatherd threw a stone and, breaking its horn, begged the goat not to tell his master.

The goat replied, "Why, you silly fellow, the horn will speak though I be silent."

# AESOP'S TIP

*Study grammar. Read your favorite stories, old and new. Understand the basics before breaking the rules.*

# WRITING PROMPTS

I. The goatherd in this fable is the son of the woman who owns the goat. Why would he be so fearful that his mother will find out about the broken horn?

II. Describe how the goat's master discovers the broken horn. What happens to the goatherd? To the goat? To the master?

III. Assume that the goatherd had been practicing at throwing stones for years. Describe his reaction when the goat's horn broke. Describe how it affected his stone throwing after it happened.

IV. Write about another character who attempted to hide something that could not be hidden.

V. Write a short story from the point of view of the goat.

# THE BOYS AND THE FROGS

Some boys were playing near a pond when they saw a number of frogs in the water and began to pelt them with stones. They killed several of them when one of the frogs, lifting his head out of the water, cried out, "Please stop! What is sport to you is death to us."

# AESOP'S TIP

*Throw stones at the frogs in your stories. Throw boulders and mountains and planets. Create ruthless situations for your protagonists so we can appreciate their hard-earned victories. Show how your characters create, remove, or avoid conflict so we can learn about their personalities.*

# WRITING PROMPTS

I. Rewrite *The Boys and the Frogs* as a revenge story. Either justify the boys' actions or allow the frogs to avenge their dead kinsmen.

II. Instead of allowing the frog to speak, give the frog a supernatural ability that can convey his message.

III. Write a fable where the three frogs represent larger concepts. For example, one frog represents greed, one represents anger, and one represents justice.

IV. Something is special about this pond. Describe what makes it notable.

V. Expand the story to include two new settings. Consider adding where the boys were coming from or where the frogs might go to hide.

VI. Write a dialog between two of the boys before they started throwing stones.

# THE RIVERS AND THE SEA

The rivers joined together to complain to the sea, saying, "Why is it that when we flow into your tides, so potable and sweet, you work in us such a change and make us salty and unfit to drink?"

The sea, perceiving that they intended to throw the blame on him, said, "Stop your flow into me, and you will not be made briny."

# AESOP'S TIP

*Collaboration shapes projects. If you work with anyone, expect the result to reflect their efforts as much as your own. Storytellers need not be solitary creatures. Do not be alarmed when someone influences your work.*

# WRITING PROMPTS

I.   Use *The Rivers and the Sea* to create a new set of characters that tell the same story. Consider using children for the rivers and a strict boarding school for the sea.

II.  Write a story where one of the rivers takes the sea up on its advice. It ceases to flow into the sea. How does this affect the river? What is the effect on the sea?

III. Write this fable as an epistolary. First write a letter to the sea from one of the rivers. Then, write a response from the sea.

IV.  Write this as a short story from the point of view of the sea.

V.   Write another story using a river as a main character.

VI.  A boatman floats down one of these rivers every season. Tell about one of his journeys.

# THE SHEPHERD AND THE SEA

A shepherd, keeping watch over his sheep near the shore, saw the sea every day and wished to sail upon it as a trader. He sold all his flock, invested it in a cargo of dates, and set sail.

Before he could leave harbor, a great tempest came on. Because the ship was in danger of sinking, he threw all his merchandise overboard and barely escaped with his life in the empty ship.

Not long afterward, when someone passed by and observed the unruffled calm of the sea, he interrupted him and said, "It is again in want of dates, and therefore looks quiet."

# AESOP'S TIP

*In times of trouble, return to the basics. There is no harm in writing what you know. When you feel blocked, work on the basics. Complete a fable prompt. Write a letter. Make a list. Throw the dates overboard.*

# WRITING PROMPTS

I. Give the man a reason for wanting to leave his flock in favor of the open sea.

II. Tell the story of the observer at the end of the fable. After the shepherd's clever remark, will the observer learn or might he make the same decision as the shepherd?

III. Give the shepherd a successful rival who had gone to sea years earlier. What happens when they meet again?

IV. Write a story using the the line, "It is again in want of dates, and therefore looks quiet."

V. Write a short story from the point of view of Poseidon. Focus on the conflict between the man and the god.

# THE LION AND THE BOAR

On a summer day, when the great heat induced a general thirst among the beasts, a lion and a boar came at the same moment to a small well to drink. They fiercely disputed which of them should drink first, and were soon engaged in the agonies of a mortal combat.

When they stopped to catch their breath, they saw some vultures waiting in the distance to feast on the one that should fall first. They at once made up their quarrel, saying, "It is better for us to make friends than to become the food of crows or vultures."

# AESOP'S TIP

*When a lion comes to a small well, readers yawn. When a boar appears, we have a conflict. When the crows arrive, we have a story. Friction creates conflict. Conflict creates stories. If your scene lacks motion, add friction.*

# WRITING PROMPTS

I. Assume that the vulture had feasted earlier that day and had come to the well knowing there might be a dispute. Tell the story from her point of view.

II. Who drank first in the end? Why? Write about what happened after this quarrel was resolved.

III. When this same meeting happened later in the summer, how did the lion and the boar greet each other? Did each come alone again?

IV. Write a short story from the point of view of the vultures. Consider writing about the first time the vultures discovered this well.

V. Write a set of rules that might be posted by the side of the well. Do these rules encourage order or do they ensure chaos? Who wrote them?

# THE EAGLE AND THE ARROW

An eagle sat on a lofty rock, watching the movements of a hare whom he sought to make his prey. An archer, who saw the eagle from a place of concealment, took an accurate aim and wounded him mortally.

The eagle gave one look at the arrow that had entered his heart and saw in that single glance that its feathers had been furnished by himself. "It is a double grief to me," he exclaimed, "that I should perish by an arrow feathered from my own wings."

# AESOP'S TIP

*Details can describe appearance, character, urgency, motive, or history. The best details accomplish several at once. Create each description as the fletcher created the arrow.*

# WRITING PROMPTS

I. Tell the story from the hunter's point of view. Assume she knew that this eagle was the same that had provided its feathers for her arrows.

II. The hare knew all along what was going to happen. Describe how it invented such a plan.

III. Create a story that other eagles tell their young about what happened that day.

IV. The hunter has a warrant out for her arrest in a nearby town. Describe what she did to merit this.

V. Write a newspaper article describing this event.

VI. Describe how the eagle's feather might have ended up in the hunter's quiver.

# THE WIDOW AND THE SHEEP

A certain poor widow had one solitary sheep. At shearing time, wishing to take his fleece and to avoid expense, she sheared him herself, but used the shears so unskillfully that with the fleece she sheared the flesh.

The sheep, writhing with pain, said, "Why do you hurt me so? What weight can my blood add to the wool? If you want my flesh, there is the butcher, who will kill me in an instant; but if you want my fleece and wool, there is the shearer, who will shear and not hurt me."

# AESOP'S TIP

*In editing, a second set of eyes is best. Do your best before asking for help, but never be afraid to approach another butcher or shearer with your story.*

# WRITING PROMPTS

I.   What was the story behind the widow's husband's death?

II.  Why did the widow have one sheep? Was this a common possession or would it have made her wealthy in her society?

III. Write the same fable in modern times. Instead of a sheep, write about something that you can find in your own home.

IV.  Write a short story from the point of view of the widow.

V.   Tell the same story without using a widow or a sheep.

VI.  One of the following nights, the sheep disappeared. Describe what happened.

# THE MOUSE, THE FROG, AND THE HAWK

A mouse, who always lived on the land, by an unlucky chance formed an intimate acquaintance with a frog. The frog, intent on mischief, bound the foot of the mouse tightly to his own. Thus joined together, the frog first of all led his friend the mouse to the meadow where they were accustomed to find their food, then to the pool in which he lived. There, he jumped in, dragging the mouse with him.

The frog enjoyed the water and swam about with pride, as if he had done a good deed. The unhappy mouse was soon suffocated by the water, and his dead body floated about on the surface, tied to the foot of the frog.

A hawk observed it and, pouncing upon it with his talons, carried it aloft. The frog, being still fastened to the leg of the mouse, was also carried off a prisoner and was eaten by the hawk.

# AESOP'S TIP

*Write your first draft all at once if you can. Focus on the details of the characters. Once you have finished, take a step back from your work. An eagle-eye view helps identify potential story arcs that are not immediately evident.*

# WRITING PROMPTS

I. Write this as a story from the point of view of the hawk.

II. Write this as a story from the point of view of the frog.

III. Write a story based on the fable where the characters are part of a hunting party that got lost in a forest.

IV. Write another story using the same moral. For an extra challenge, style your story in the manner of the fable, using only three characters.

V. Write a news article inspired by the events in the fable.

VI. Write a letter from a someone who happened to see one of the parts of this fable and ended up with a completely different view of what happened.

# THE TWO DOGS

A man had two dogs: a hound, trained to assist him in his sports, and a house-dog, taught to watch the house.

When the man returned home after a good day's sport, he always gave the house-dog a large share of his spoil. The hound, feeling much aggrieved at this, reproached his companion, saying, "It annoys me that I work all day for this food while you, who do not assist in the chase, luxuriate on the fruits of my exertions."

The house-dog replied, "Do not blame me, my friend, but find fault with the master, who has not taught me to labor, but to depend for subsistence on the labor of others."

# AESOP'S TIP

*Identify what you admire about your favorite authors, your favorite poets, your favorite artists. Learn their lessons. Study their histories. Learn from the masters, but appreciate even those who do not directly influence your work.*

# WRITING PROMPTS

I. The hound was not pleased with the house-dog's response. Instead, he formed a plan to teach the house-dog that individuals can rise above the limitations of their upbringing. Write about what happened. Was the hound or the house-dog right in the end?

II. Describe why the man chose the hound as his hunting companion.

III. Describe why the man chose the house-dog as his watchdog.

IV. Write a story about these two dogs who met in other circumstances. If they had never met their current master, how would they interact?

V. Tell a story that the master might relay to his children about the importance of a house-dog.

# THE OLD WOMAN AND
# THE WINE-JAR

An old woman found an empty jar that had once been full of prime old wine and still retained the fragrant smell of its former contents.

She greedily placed it several times to her nose, and drawing it backwards and forwards said, "Delicious! How nice must the wine itself have been; it leaves behind such sweet perfume!"

# AESOP'S TIP

*The memory of a good story outlives even the books where it was written. Find classic stories in literature. Appreciate the lingering perfume.*

# WRITING PROMPTS

I.   Write the story of the wine-jar. Where did it come from? Who made the wine?

II.  Write about what the old woman did with the jar after enjoying its scent.

III. The woman was entranced by the simple wine-jar. Because of this excitement, her enthusiasm became legendary. Write about another item for which she displays similar excitement.

IV.  Write a short story from the point of view of the old woman's best friend.

V.   Describe a night in the history of the empty jar, perhaps from a time when it was full of wine.

# THE HUNTSMAN AND
# THE FISHERMAN

A huntsman, returning with his dogs from the field, fell in by chance with a fisherman who was bringing home a basket well laden with fish.

The huntsman wished to have the fish, and the fisherman experienced an equal longing for the contents of the game-bag. They soon agreed to exchange the produce of their day's sport.

Each was so well pleased with his bargain that they made for some time the same exchange day after day. Finally a neighbor said to them, "If you go on in this way, you will soon destroy by frequent use the pleasure of your exchange, and each will again wish to retain the fruits of his own sport."

# AESOP'S TIP

*Once you have completed the first draft of a story, let it sit. Abstain from editing it for a month or two until the words have left your recent memory. The time will allow you to focus on the work as if it were new.*

# WRITING PROMPTS

I. Assume the neighbor also had something to sell. Explain the neighbor's story and why he wanted the huntsman and the fisherman to trade less frequently.

II. The fisherman often fell prey to similar situations. Write about another time the fisherman compulsively repeated a task.

III. Write about how the addition of fish to their diet changed life for the family of the huntsman.

IV. Describe a day in the life of the neighbor, of the huntsman, and of the fisherman.

V. Write about how the addition of good game meat to their diet changed life for the community of the fisherman.

VI. Write a short story from the point of view of the huntsman.

# ADDITIONAL FABLES

# THE LIONESS IN LOVE

A lioness once fell in love with a beautiful young man. She told the gentleman's parents of her affection and asked for his hand in marriage. The parents, who did not want to give up their son to the lion, did not want to anger the queen of beasts.

They said to the lioness, "We are honored by your request and appreciate the depth of your affection for our son. Still, we worry that you might tear him to pieces with the vehemence of your affection. We ask that you consider trimming your claws and removing your teeth before proposing such a marriage to our darling boy."

So deep was her love that she did trim her claws and remove her teeth. When she came back to propose once more, the parents and young man laughed at her and said, "Do your worst!"

# WRITING PROMPTS

I.   How did the young man and the lioness meet? Were the feelings mutual before the lioness met with his parents?

II.  Write a letter from the lioness to the young man's parents proposing the marriage. Write a second letter from after the fable takes place.

III. Write another ending to this fable.

IV.  Describe what happens after this fable ends. Does the young man ever get married? What happens to his parents?

V.   How did the young man's parents meet?

VI.  Perhaps the lioness had a reputation for causing harm in the past. Write a story from years ago that might have caused the parents in this fable to react the way that they did.

# THE WIND AND THE SUN

The wind and the sun were disputing over which was stronger. As they fought, a man in a long coat walked by.

"The strongest," the two agreed, "will be the one who can make this man remove his coat." The wind offered to go first and the sun hid behind a cloud.

The wind gusted and blew, but the harder it tried, the tighter the man drew his coat. Exhausted, the wind died down and allowed the sun to come out.

As the sun shone calmly down and warmed the air, the man unfastened his coat and tossed it over his shoulder.

# WRITING PROMPTS

I.  What spurred the argument between the sun and the wind? Have they fought before?

II. Describe a situation where the wind might prove itself strongest. It might challenge the moon, the sea, or the rain.

III. The man in the story was happy to have brought a coat that morning. Describe the rest of his day.

IV. Rewrite this story using humans to represent the sun and the wind. Maintain the moral, kindness affects more than severity.

V.  Create another competition between the sun and another elemental force.

VI. How would this fable differ if this man did not have a coat at the beginning of the challenge? Would the sun still have won the dispute?

# THE WORKER AND THE NIGHTENGALE

A worker greatly enjoyed the song of the nightengale whenever he closed his eyes to sleep. Because of this, he decided to catch the bird so that he might forever enjoy its song.

Once he captured the bird, it responded, "We nightengales never sing in cages."

"Then I will eat you!" said the man, "for I hear your meat is fine."

"If you free me, I will tell you three things more valuable than my meat," said the bird.

The worker freed the bird and listened as it said, "The first thing: never trust the words of a captive. The second: keep what you have. The third: do not regret that which is gone forever."

With that, the bird flew away.

# WRITING PROMPTS

I. This has happened to the nightengale before. Describe the first time the bird was captured and how he dealt with the situation.

II. What other advice might the bird have given to the worker so that it could be free? Tell the story from the point of view of the worker's daughter, having heard the story herself as a child.

III. Rewrite this story using two new characters in a modern setting. Be sure that the moral remains the same in the new version.

IV. Write an alternate ending to this fable. What could the worker have said to the bird instead of letting it go? How might this have changed everything?

V. Describe the day when the worker first heard about the fine meat that birds can provide.

# THE FOX WITHOUT A TAIL

A fox became entangled in a snare in the woods. She was able to free herself, but lost most of her tail in the process.

After a few months, she called a meeting with all of the other foxes in the area and said, "We should all dispose of our tails. They are an emcumberance at best and provide little real value in our lives."

To this, another fox responded, "I do not think you would be giving the same advice if you still had your tail."

# WRITING PROMPTS

I. Write a dialogue between two other foxes in attendance at this meeting.

II. If the fox without the tail was the queen of the forest, she might have crafted an edict requiring the loss of all tails. Write a story where this was the case.

III. Rewrite this fable so that the fox without the tail is the protagonist. Consider what might make the other foxes more empathetic to her request.

IV. Write about the hunter who placed the snare.

V. What happened to the tail after the fox lost it? Tell the story of the next two people who encountered this lost appendage.

VI. Rewrite this fable as a dramatic mystery story.

# THE OLD MAN AND DEATH

An old worker, doubled over from age and weariness, was gathering firewood in a forest when he cried out, "If only death would come and take me!"

Out of the darkness, a skeleton approached and asked, "What would you have of me, mortal?"

The man shivered and said, "Could you help me carry this firewood?"

# WRITING PROMPTS

I.   Write the story of how Death might have found his way into the forest that day.

II.   Write the man's journal entry from later that night, after coming so close to his own death. Then, create an entry from the night before.

III.   Write about the day when these two characters met again.

IV.   Who did Death visit next? Write about the next interaction someone had with this skeleton.

V.   Someone was waiting for the man's return. Write the story of his wife, son, or friend who was collecting firewood on the other side of the man's house.

# BELLING THE CAT

All the mice in the area gathered to discuss their greatest foe, the house cat. One of the mice said, "The biggest danger that we face comes from the quiet and nimble nature of our enemy. If we had a way to set off an alarm when he was near, we would never have to worry again!"

Another mouse said, "We should tie a bell to his collar. That would solve the problem in an instant."

Someone asked who would attach the bell to the cat's collar.

The oldest mouse in the room replied, "It is easy to suggest impossible solutions."

# WRITING PROMPTS

I.   Figure out a way to solve the problem of belling the cat and write it into the dialogue in the fable.

II.  Why does the old mouse seem so surly? Create a story from his youth that might explain his repugnant demeanor.

III. Write about a similar meeting where the cats discuss their own preditors and prey.

IV.  Rewrite this fable so that it takes place during the renaissance using characters you might have learned about in history class.

V.   Create a twist in the plot after the fable ends.

VI.  The cat might have heard this entire conversation. Because of her quiet and nimble nature, she might have snuck up on the oldest of the mice and waited for the right moment. Write about this meeting from her point of view.

# THE YOUNG THIEF AND HIS MOTHER

A young thief was caught in a devious act of theft and was sentenced to execution for his crimes. When asked if he had any final requests, the man asked to see his mother one last time.

When she was brought before him, the man pulled her close and bit hard at her ear. The guards pulled her to safety and she cried out, asking why he would do such a vile act.

The thief responded, "I came home as a child after stealing something small and you laughed at me, never correcting my actions. It is because of you that I am here today."

# WRITING PROMPTS

I.  Describe the devious act of theft that warranted the thief's cruel sentence.

II. Write the arrest document that the security guard handed in when he delivered the prisoner. Use the guard's vernacular to describe how the thief was found and the evidence that proved his guilt.

III. Write a letter from the mother to her son from a month preceeding the theft in the fable.

IV. Tell this story from the point of view of the man who was robbed. What was his involvement with the young thief before and after this fable took place?

V.  Rewrite this fable to present a different moral. If possible, use the same thief, the same devious act, and the same mother as described in the original.

# THE WOODSMAN AND THE SERPENT

A woodsman was on his way home when he saw a dark serpent lying in the snow by a tree. The woodsman picked up the serpent and held it to his chest, keeping it warm for the rest of his walk home.

Once inside his cabin, he set the snake by the fire and went about making dinner for the two of them. One of the woodsman's children saw the serpent and approached just as it was waking up from the cold sleep. It opened its mouth wide and was about to bite the child when the woodsman split the serpent in twain with his axe.

"No gratitude from the wicked," said the woodsman.

# WRITING PROMPTS

I. Write about how the serpent fell into such a state beneath the tree during the winter.

II. Describe what the child might have done to deserve the attention of the snake. Consider that the two had met before and that the cruelty of the child might have warrented action from the serpent.

III. Write a letter from the woodsman to someone else describing his interaction with the snake. Maybe the man is superstitious about such animals. Write about why he might feel this way.

IV. Who taught the woodsman to use his axe? Tell that person's story.

V. Rewrite this story using modern characters in an unusual setting.

# THE ROOSTER AND THE PEARL

A rooster was strutting up and down near the hen-house when he spotted a small gleaming object beneath the straw. "Wow," he cried, "that treasure belongs to me!"

When he uncovered it from the straw, he stepped back and said, "A pearl would be a wonderful treasure to some, but I would rather have a single barley-corn."

# WRITING PROMPTS

I.  Tell the story of the person who lost the pearl near the hen-house.
    Focus on the story of the person and the story of the pearl.

II. Because he gave it so little value, the rooster might have left the
    pearl where it was, he might have given it to someone else, or he
    might have buried it under the straw. Where happened to it after
    the rooster walked away?

III. Tell the story of why the rooster was walking in that specific
     location that morning. Create something unexpected in this
     story.

IV. The farmer who owned the rooster comes from a very poor
    family and values the eggs from the hens more than anything in
    the world. What might he do if he found a pearl on his farm?

V.  Three children were working near the hen-houses later that
    afternoon. Describe what might happen if one of the children
    found the pearl and did not want the others to find out.

# THE LION'S SHARE

A lion, a fox, a dog, and a wolf went hunting together in the forest. After a long day, they came across a stag. Each of the animals leapt together and killed their prey at once.

"What should we do with it now?" asked the fox.

"Divide the meat into four parts," said the lion.

"And who gets what?" asked the wolf.

"I will take one share as king of the forest," said the lion, "and another as the one who determined the spoils." The other animals drooled, but the lion continued. "And one more is my share for my part in the chase. And I dare any of you to try to take the last piece from me."

"You can share the labors of the great, but never the spoils," the fox said to the dog as they walked away in hunger.

# WRITING PROMPTS

I. Imagine that the three other hunters did not accept the lion's decision. Write about what happens after this fable ends, assuming that the other animals work together.

II. What led the stag to the forest that day? Tell the story of his life.

III. Back at the lion's den, there was another story taking place. Describe what happened.

IV. Rewrite this story as a fantasy. You can include animals as characters, but consider creating something entirely new.

V. Write about the lion's greatest victory in his own words.

VI. Describe the lion's rule from the point of view of the other animals that joined him on the hunt.

# THE WOLF AND THE CRANE

A wolf was gorging himself on the spoils of a recent hunt when a bone became lodged in his throat. He groaned and whined to everyone who would listen until finally he came across a crane.

"Please help," said the wolf, "and I will reward you greatly."

The crane told him to lie on his side and, when he did, stuck her head down his throat to remove the bone. Once it was free, she pulled her head out and said, "I have helped you, might I have the reward that you promised?"

The wolf said, "You have stuck your head down the throat of a wolf and still you live. Surely that is reward enough."

# WRITING PROMPTS

I.  Use this wolf in another story. In this new tale, show how the wolf interacts with other animals in the forest. Create depth to his personality by showing more than one aspect of his personality in your story. He might help one animal but hurt another.

II. What other notable events has the crane encountered in her time in the forest?

III. Write a poem using this fable as inspiration.

IV. Combine the wolf in this fable with characters in another fable. Write the story to show how the fables might change given different circumstances.

V.  A mouse witnessed the events in this fable and it changed her life forever. Write an opinion article from this mouse describing her thoughts on wolves in the forest.

# WRITING EXERCISES

# ON LETTERS

1. You have been away on vacation for a full month and will be heading home soon. Write a letter to the person who was watching your house . Let her know a little about your trip, but also include some of your upcoming plans for when you return.

2. The man you never expected to see again just sent you an email. What did it say?

3. Aunt Laurie has asked that you craft a letter on behalf of the whole family this holiday season. She does not want you to mention the recent court battle, but understands that it has been on the news and that some people might have questions. It should be okay to mention cousin Burt's "accident," but do not put too much blame on him for ruining Thanksgiving dinner.

4. Treasure maps always preceed adventure. That's what Jacob thought when he opened the scroll he found in his grandfather's attic. Write the contents of this scroll.

5. "It ain't easy running from Johnny Law." Sometimes even a fugitive wants to write home. You may want to be cryptic as you write this letter. Who knows what the authorities might glean from the words if you aren't careful?

6. This letter was intercepted heading to an important diplomat at the consulate. It describes the current living situation of a single family, but sheds light on a deeper issue. Write this letter.

7. When she landed on the Northern tip of the island, she said that the new society would be governed by justice. That was over 100 years ago now. What did she lay out in her first open letter to the settlers that travelled aboard her ships?

8. Write a letter containing a mother's aspirations for her child. Include hints as to why she might be writing the letter at all.

9. One man wrote down his fears in a series of letters to his son. Write two of these letters.

10. Write a letter containing at least one of the following lines:

   11. *I expect you already know the reason for this letter.*

   12. *He can never know of this.*

   13. *Congratulations on another successful release.*

   14. *Who do you think you are?*

   15. *Third door on the right. It's the one with the scratch marks down the middle.*

   16. *We sent a single envelope with all of the documents she requested.*

   17. *I hope this reaches you.*

   18. *Tell him that he's the most important person in my life.*

   19. *I will be staying indefinately.*

# ON INSTRUCTIONS

1. Mme. Boverau hosts the finest parties in the country. Nothing is left to chance on the afternoon of the event. Because of her great preperation, little is left to chance. Write one of her lists of rules. This might be for the chef, the entertainment, or the serving staff.

2. Instructions often appear in children's literature and have a history in fairy tales. Write a set of fantastic rules for a child in one of these stories.

3. Create a set of rules for the worst public pool in the universe.

4. You have been granted the position of parole officer and judge over the newest batch of recently freed prisoners. Write guidelines for these new charges. How must they prove their ability to function in society? What freedoms are they allowed? Which are denied?

5. The first Mars colony needs laws. Write five or ten new laws that will be presented to the colonists for ratification. Consider the atmosphere, the recent burst of thefts, and the citizens that have built their homes there.

6. Create a page of safety instructions for adventurers heading to the nearby ruins. What traps might they avoid? What animals might they spot on their journey? What should they do with the relics or treasures that they find?

7. Write ten rules for a classroom without using the words "do not" in your list.

8. There is a mystery to be solved. What rules should be followed by the detective in the story to make sure she uncovers all of the

clues necessary to solve the crime? What about the mastermind behind the theft?

9. Write a story where the protagonist fails to follow an important instruction and must face severe consequenses.

10. Write a story where the protagonist tries to warn a group of people using a set of rules. What happens when someone in the group breaks one? How does the protagonist respond?

11. Write a story where the protagonist breaks a seemingly important rule and is rewarded for it.

# ON MYTHOLOGY

For these exercises, you will be creating myths to explain specific occurances. In Greek mythology, the god Helios drives his firey chariot across the sky to bring daylight. Selene does the same with the moon during the night. Explain the events below by creating a new mythology of your own device.

- Why the sun rises

- Why the moon takes different shapes

- The ebb and flow of the tides

- The existence of mountains

- Why a specific river flows south

- The orgin of a flow

- Why birds sing

- Why evergreen trees have needles

- Why thunder crashes during storms

- The existance or name of a specific body of water (Lake Michigan, The Pacific Ocean, even the pond in the back of your house)

- The existence of the city where you live

- Why you were given your name

- A prophecy for the next great world event

- The origin of the world

- The first temple created by humans

- Life on other planets (or why there is no life on other planets)

# ON SELF REFLECTION

1.  Begin by keeping a daily journal this week. Focus on concrete details and experiences for each entry. Briefly describe the people you encounter, the places you visit, and the things that you do. After a full week, go back to your first entry and write a short essay about one of your experiences.

2.  Start a daily drawing journal. Instead of writing entries about your day, take ten or twenty minutes to draw a single image as your entry. This project can be done over the course of a month or a year. Once you have finished, revise and re-create your favorite images in a new medium.

3.  Write a letter to yourself from the future. From this perspective, you can advise yourself of lessons learned, warn of potential risks, and encourage the pursuit of new opportunities.

4.  What did you dream of becoming when you were a child? Write a short story where you are the protagonist in your childhood dream.

5.  Make a list of your best and worst qualities. Once the list is complete, create characters who represent each list. Write about a time when these two characters meet. If the scene works, expand it into a story.

6.  Find your favorite book and make a list of the main characters that it includes. Break down each character by the way they interact with each other. Once you have a strong understanding of these traits, write a story where you meet one of these characters in a setting from the book. Focus on maintaining the realism of your own character and the one you chose from the book.

7.  Create an alter ego for yourself. Write about a day in the life of this other self.

# ON STORYTELLING

1. Start with the last line. Write a list of five declaritive statements. Each should surprise you and make you smile. Now, build a story that ends with one of these sentences. This story does not have a length requirement. Instead, this exercise encourages you to change the way you think about storytelling.

2. Make a list of at least ten times in your life when you have been vigorously active. Find a friend, choose one of the items on your list, and tell him about what happened. Focus on creating an engaging environment. Consider your movement in the story and the movement you use to tell the story.

3. Tell a story about the loudest thing you have ever heard. Include at least two other characters in your story, whether they were present at the time of the event or not.

4. For a full day, take notes. Take notes on what you do, where you are, who you meet, and what you talk about. Once you have finished, create a story from your notes. To find segments that will make good stories, take notice of times when you were excited, annoyed, or challenged in some way.

5. Ask someone to tell you a story that you have told him in the past. As you listen, be aware of the moments that are described. The way the story is told will help you understand the way you tell stories.

6. Find a way to tell a story without

   - talking directly to a person.
   - writing more than a sentence at a time.
   - having to be present at the time of the story being told.
   - the audience being able to identify you as the storyteller.
   - taking credit for the story you are telling.

# STORYTELLING
# GAMES AND
# EXERCISES

# FALABORATE

This collaborative storytelling game is fun for groups. Unlike most games, all of the participants play cooperatively.

**ESTIMATED TIME:** 120 MINUTES
**PLAYERS:** 2 - 30
**FOCUS:** TEAMWORK
**WHAT YOU NEED:** WRITING MATERIALS

1.  Choose a Game Master (GM) from the participants. The GM will be the one who writes down the story and has final say on whether group decisions are added or omitted. The GM can be removed by popular vote at any time by a 51 percent majority.

2.  Decide on the moral of the story. Everyone is invited to suggest morals and to offer advice on why a specific moral should or should not be included.

3.  Decide where the story will take place. Choose a setting and a time period (if that is important to your story). If your group needs ideas, check under the "Rolling a Fable" section for potential locations to include in your story.

4.  Choose characters. These can be anything or anyone from traditional fables or from modern media. Foxes can meet superheros. Venus can remix an Opera into a bass-heavy dance mix.

5.  Start laying out the plot. What happens in the story? Who

meets whom? What happens? Make an outline together. It may help to break the outline into segments at this point.

6. Before breaking off to write, be sure to agree on a single point-of-view, setting, and character names (in addition to everything you discussed before).

7. Have everyone choose a segment of the outline to write themselves. Everyone will write for ten or fifteen minutes and come back together to share the story from start to finish.

8. The group should talk about each section and whether it is necessary to the story. What stays? What goes?

9. The GM will compile the story into a single piece and read the final story aloud to everyone.

Victory!

# POLYDICTIC

Our best descriptions serve more than one purpose.

"The lion roared," states an action. "The mouse jumped at the sound of the lion's roar," shows a relationship between two characters and describes action. Polydictic is a game where every sentence serves more than one purpose.

**ESTIMATED TIME:** 60 MINUTES
**PLAYERS:** 2+
**FOCUS:** LATERAL THINKING
**WHAT YOU NEED:** WRITING MATERIALS

*Setup:* With larger groups of players, consider nominating someone as a full-time editor for the Polydictic story. This person will make corrections and edit the document as everyone works.

1. The first and only unbreakable rule of Polydictic is that every sentence needs to serve more than one purpose.

2. The first player (chosen at random) writes the first sentence in a story.

3. The next player writes the last sentence of a story on the same piece of paper.

4. After the first and last sentences of the story are written, players take turns coming up with the connecting story. Remember rule

number 1! Every line must serve more than one purpose.

5.  Players are encouraged to ask each other questions and defend their sentence choices vocally.

**Example:**
Player 1 writes the opening sentence: "The mouse jumped at the sound of the lion's roar." Player 2 writes the closing line: "His voice was still higher than most, but his valor and title earned the respect of every animal in the forest." The next player starts connecting the first and last lines with a new sentence of her own.

6.  This is a collaborative game. Everyone is working on the same story. For best results, start simple and be patient. It takes practice to play Polydictic well, but the stories you create will be worth the effort.

# STORY GUESSING GAME FOR TWO

The Story Guessing Game relies on your storytelling abilities as much as your knowledge of Aesop's fables. The two player version is simple to learn and can be completed in an hour.

**ESTIMATED TIME:** 60 MINUTES
**PLAYERS:** 2
**FOCUS:** SHORT STORIES
**WHAT YOU NEED:** WRITING MATERIALS

1. Each player chooses a fable and writes his choice on a piece of paper. This choice is hidden and will only be shown to the opposing player at the end of the round.

2. Each player writes a story based on his chosen fable. The length of the story and duration of the writing time is determined by both players before the round begins.

To maintain a 60 minute timeline, we recommend short fiction of no more than 500 words and a writing time of 10 minutes. Players can agree to longer word counts and timelines if they choose.

3. Once the writing time is up, players swap and read each other's stories.

4. Once they have finished reading, each player will guess the fable that inspired their opponent's story. The player with the higher score at the end of three rounds, wins.

**SCORING:**

+1 point if you guess your opponent's story

+2 points if you both guess correctly

-10 points each if neither player is able to guess correctly

# STORY GUESSING GAME FOR MORE

For this Story Guessing Game, designed for more than two players, choose one person to work as the Game Master (this could be an instructor or another non-playing writer).

**ESTIMATED TIME:** 60-120 MINUTES
**PLAYERS:** 3 - 30
**FOCUS:** SHORT STORIES
**WHAT YOU NEED:** WRITING MATERIALS

1.  Every participant should choose a fable from the 35 included in *Write with Lions* and should give her choice to the Game Master (GM). The GM writes these choices down next to the name of the writer and keeps this information secret.

2.  Every participant writes a story based on the chosen fable. Stories should not exceed 500 words. Once the stories are completed, they are handed to the GM for review and distribution.

3.  Once all of the stories are handed in, the GM distributes them randomly to the participants, ensuring that the original writer does not recieve her own story for review.

4.  Each participant reads the story that has been handed to her and, on a seperate piece of paper, writes a guess at the fable that inspired the story.

5. Once a reader finishes guessing their first piece, she is encouraged to trade with other readers. All participants can read and guess at as many stories as they can before the time runs out. Each reader keeps track of her own guesses until the end, when she hands in her guess sheet to the GM.

6. The GM reviews the guess-sheets and determines the winner based on the point system below.

**SCORING:**
+1 point for the READER for every correct guess
+1 point for the WRITER for every time their fable is guessed correctly
+5 points for the READER with the most correct guesses
-2 points for the WRITER with the most correctly guessed fable

# YOUR ASSIGNMENT . . .

"This statue was made by one of you men. If we lions knew how to erect statues, you would see the man placed under the paw of the lion." The lion noted that stories change depending on the view of the storyteller. Your Assignment. . . plays with the same idea.

**ESTIMATED TIME:** 30 MINUTES
**PLAYERS:** 2
**FOCUS:** ABSTRACT THINKING
**WHAT YOU NEED:** WRITING MATERIALS

1. The youngest player writes first (Player 1). Player 2 chooses a writing prompt from *Write with Lions* and determines two additional writing restrictions to impose upon Player 1.

2. Player 1 responds by choosing a writing prompt from *Write with Lions* for Player 2 and imposes an additional two writing restrictions as she sees fit.

**Example:**
Player 2 chooses Writing Prompt II from "The Two Dogs" as a challenge for Player 1. She also decides that the response must be written in first-person and that the entire piece cannot be longer than four sentences.

3. Each player begins writing using the prompts and restrictions set up by the opposing player. This segment does not have a predetermined time limit unless the players choose to impose one.

4. Once the responses are finished, each player reads her work aloud.

5. This continues until one or both players are unable to complete the assignment given by their opponent.

**SCORING:**
This game does not keep score. It continues until one or both players are unable to complete an assignment. The player who gives the un-finishable assignment must, herself, complete the same assignment in order to claim victory.

**Example:**
Player 2 assigns Writing Prompt II from "The Two Dogs" as a challenge for Player 1. She also decides that the response must be written in first-person and the entire piece cannot exceed four sentences in length. If Player 1 submits a response exceeding four sentences, Player 2 has the option of completing the same challenge. If she does, she wins!

# YOUR GROUP
# ASSIGNMENT . . .

"This statue was made by one of you men. If we lions knew how to erect statues, you would see the man placed under the paw of the lion." The lion noted that stories change depending on the view of the storyteller. Your Group Assignment. . . plays with the same idea.

**ESTIMATED TIME:** 50 MINUTES
**PLAYERS:** 3 - 30
**FOCUS:** ABSTRACT THINKING
**WHAT YOU NEED:** WRITING MATERIALS

1.  Choose a Game Master (GM). He chooses a fable and reads it aloud to the group.

2.  Each player writes down one writing restriction and gives it to the GM. Restrictions can be broad or specific. If you need ideas, consider some of the examples below.

**Examples:**
Write in the form of haiku.
Include at least one historical allusion.
Write in first-person point-of-view.
Avoid mentioning the name of the protagonist.
Use the characters in the fable, but tell a different story.

3.  The GM chooses three restrictions at random from the ones written by the players and reads them aloud to the participants.

4. Everyone writes using the fable and restrictions as guidelines. This writing time should not exceed fifteen minutes.

5. Each participant reads hisr story aloud. Cheering, laughter, hissing, and howling are encouraged during this part.

6. Once everyone has finished reading, players choose two of their favorite stories and write their choices down. They hand their choices to the GM, who tallies up the votes.

7. The GM takes the top three stories and awards them with first, second, and third place based on stories that recieved the most votes.

8. For an additional level of fun, take the top story from this game and save it for the next time you play. The GM will read this story during step 5, and the participants will be allowed to vote for this story, too. If this story wins during the next competition, the GM wins the game.

# ROLLING A FABLE

Use a deck of cards or a set of dice to create your own fable. This is a game that can be played alone or in a group. Roll the dice to determine which characters appear in your story, where it takes place, and whether it should include a specific moral.

**ESTIMATED TIME:** AS LONG AS YOU WANT
**PLAYERS:** 1 OR MORE
**FOCUS:** DESTROYING WRITERS BLOCK
**WHAT YOU NEED:** WRITING MATERIALS, DICE

Two dice determine which characters to use in your story. Add up the result of your roll and use the chart below.

| Roll | Characters |
|------|------------|
| 2 | Fox and Sheep |
| 3 | Hunter and Lion |
| 4 | Frog, Boy, and Turtle |
| 5 | Two Mice |
| 6 | Weasel and Mouse |
| 7 | Eagle, Traveler, and Flea |
| 8 | Widow, Frog, and Cat |
| 9 | Venus and Monkey |
| 10 | Three lions |
| 11 | Wolf and Shepherd |
| 12 | Jupiter and the Sea |

One die will determine the setting of your story. Roll only once and use the chart below.

| Roll | Setting |
|------|---------|
| 1 | On an isolated island |
| 2 | At a farm |
| 3 | In a dance hall |
| 4 | In the middle of a city |
| 5 | On the edge of a cliff |
| 6 | Your choice |

Two dice to determine the moral of the fable. Use the chart below.

| Roll | Moral or Theme |
|------|----------------|
| 2 | Harm seek, harm find |
| 3 | Dishonest words are easily spotted |
| 4 | Greed for more can destroy all |
| 5 | Treat others the way you would like to be treated |
| 6 | It is possible to mistake notoriety for fame |
| 7 | Council without help is useless |
| 8 | It is best to learn by doing |
| 9 | A bad temper is its own punishment |
| 10 | Any moral you choose |
| 11 | No moral |
| 12 | Quality trumps quantity |

# EVERYONE'S ROLLING A FABLE

Like the solitare version of Rolling a Fable, this game uses numbers to determine random story prompts. Use the charts below to determine the type of fable your team will be writing. Work with your team to write the best story possible.

**ESTIMATED TIME:** 60 MINUTES
**PLAYERS:** 3-30 (2 GROUPS)
**FOCUS:** COLLABORATION
**WHAT YOU NEED:** WRITING MATERIALS, DICE

Before you start, have the Game Master (GM) determine the length of writing time allowed to each group. We recommend 30 minutes of time to collaborate and an additional 10 minutes to write. After this time is up, both stories will be shared and the GM will choose a winner however she sees fit.

Choose the setting first. Use the chart below to determine the setting based on a single roll of the die.

| Roll | Setting |
|------|---------|
| 1 | In a complex system of underground tunnels |
| 2 | Near a rainforest |
| 3 | In the middle of the desert |
| 4 | On a small boat |
| 5 | In a busy street |
| 6 | At a temple |

Choose the characters next. Two Dice for this one.

| Roll | Characters |
|------|-----------|
| 2 | Lion and Mouse |
| 3 | Monkey and the Sea |
| 4 | Jupiter and the Fisherman |
| 5 | Three dogs |
| 6 | Wolf and Hercules |
| 7 | Mouse, Weasel, and Pig |
| 8 | Goat and Stag |
| 9 | Horse, Sheep, and Farmer |
| 10 | Hunter, Cat, and Lion |
| 11 | Two Frogs and Boy |
| 12 | Any characters you choose |

For additional challenges, use one die to determine which of the following to add to the stories. Roll twice and use both challenges!

| Roll | Challenge |
|------|-----------|
| 1 | Write in first-person point of view |
| 2 | Include trickery in your story |
| 3 | Include a moral in your story |
| 4 | Include a pocket watch and a book in your story |
| 5 | Tell the story from memory, without notes |
| 6 | No additional restriction |

# THE APARTMENTS

This game can be played alone or with many, many players. While everyone will be writing stories about the same apartment building, no two stories will be the same. The genres will vary. The characters will vary. Once the game is finished, you will have created a full building worth of stories.

**ESTIMATED TIME:** DAYS OR WEEKS
**PLAYERS:** 1 PLAYER+
**FOCUS:** CHARACTER DEVELOPMENT / PLOTTING
**WHAT YOU NEED:** WRITING MATERIALS

If you are playing this game with more than one player, it would be best to gather everyone in the same place at the start. Due to the time constraints on this game, players will not need to remain in the same place as they participate.

1.  Once you have gathered, have everyone decide on the location of your apartment building. It will work best if you choose an actual location, even if the building is vacant in reality. Choose a place with at least as many floors as you have participants. Pull up a photo of the building and show everyone the location on a map.

**Example:**
A group of four storytellers might choose a building in downtown Chicago with six stories. They found the building online and reviewed the neighborhood on the map. Everyone agreed that this would be the setting for their stories.

213

2. Determine the numbering system for the apartments in the building. You can use a fictional numbering system, just make sure that all of the participants understand how it works.

3. Every participant chooses an apartment to start with. This is the apartment that will inspire his first story.

4. For this first round, everyone has an enormous amount of freedom. Each participant can choose his own characters, genre, and plot. The only limitation is that the primary character must inhabit the apartment chosen in step 3.

5. Determine the exact deadline and rough length for the first apartment story. For longer stories, take at least a week before meeting again. If you choose to write shorter stories, try meet again the same day.

6. Once participants have completed their first stories, meet to discuss. Everyone should share their story with the rest of the participants, if possible.

7. Each player chooses another apartment. The new apartment needs to be in the same building as before, and cannot be one that was previously chosen.

8. The next round of stories can be told in the same genre and style as the first, or in a totally new style. Consider allowing the inhabitants of your new apartment to interact with the characters from other stories.

9. Continue this process until you have created enough stories to fill the entire apartment complex.

10. Trade stories with other writers. Edit, critique, and challenge the stories. Bring them together and read them. Choose your

favorites. Finish the critiques and drafting process.

11. Compile all of the stories in a single location. Consider adding these to a single website or creating your own co-authored book of short stories.

12. Success!

# WORKSHEETS AND OTHER USEFUL ITEMS

# WORKSHEET NOTES

Use these pages for brainstorming, plot development, and notes. You could photo-copy them (or find versions online at MoreKnown.com) if you don't want to mark up your copy of the book.

You know that thing teachers do sometimes, where they lay the book on a scanner and then copy it a million times so they can hand out worksheets to their classes? That's why this section exists. Maybe you're not a teacher. Maybe you just like to write. That's just fine too. You could bring them to a writing group, an eccentric dinner party, or just scribble on them as you brainstorm alone.

# CHARACTER BUILDER

Physical Characteristics

_____

_____

_____

_____

_____

Portrait

Short Introduction

Greatest Desire
Greatest Fear
Greatest Strength
Greatest Weakness

# CHARACTER BUILDER

Physical Characteristics

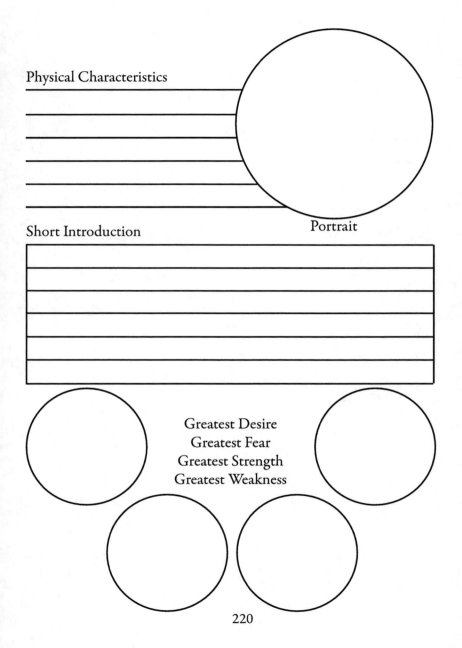

Portrait

Short Introduction

Greatest Desire
Greatest Fear
Greatest Strength
Greatest Weakness

# CHARACTER BUILDER

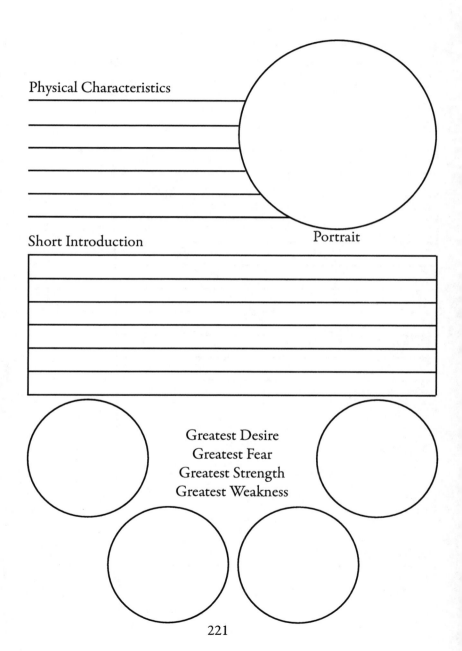

Physical Characteristics

Portrait

Short Introduction

Greatest Desire
Greatest Fear
Greatest Strength
Greatest Weakness

# KEEPING A DIARY

Keep a daily journal from the point of view of each of your main characters. This will help keep perspective as you write your story. Focus on each character's desires as you write.

# CREATING A WORLD

Wide View: Describe the world where your story takes place. Focus primarily on areas that might impact your characters in some way.
Trade: Describe how the economy works in your world.

Governments

Major Global Figures

Localized View: Describe the smaller setting where your story starts.

Major Cultural Groups

Unique Facts

# NEWSPAPER

| HEADLINE |
|---|
| ARTICLE IMAGE |

Author, with byline

# HEADLINE

ARTICLE IMAGE

ARTICLE IMAGE

ARTICLE IMAGE

# MOTIVATIONS

Character Name and Titles
(relationship to the protagonist
if applicable)

List the major desires
of the character

List  the challenges
that prevent the
character from
achieving these desires

# MOTIVATIONS

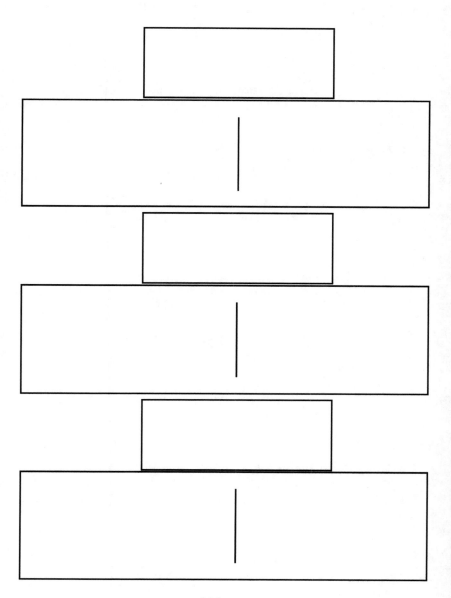

# MOTIVATIONS

# MOTIVATIONS

# PLOTTING

( Event )  [ Description ]

When creating longer stories, it helps to visualize the entire layout. Choose the main events in your story. Some will be major events that shake the foundations of the entire story; others will impact only a single character. In the descriptions, be sure to list how the event moves the story forward and which characters it affects.

# MAPS

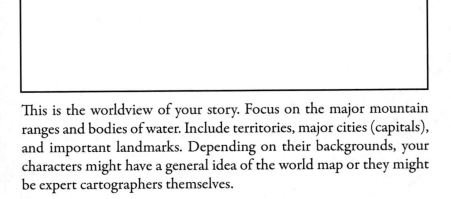

This is the worldview of your story. Focus on the major mountain ranges and bodies of water. Include territories, major cities (capitals), and important landmarks. Depending on their backgrounds, your characters might have a general idea of the world map or they might be expert cartographers themselves.

On the next page, build two smaller maps of specific areas. Focus on the settings where the majority of your action will take place. Consider the planning of the towns, villages, or cities. It might be an urban environment with millions of citizens or a rural area where only a handful of people have ever explored.

Setting 1

Setting 2

237

# FABLE BUILDER

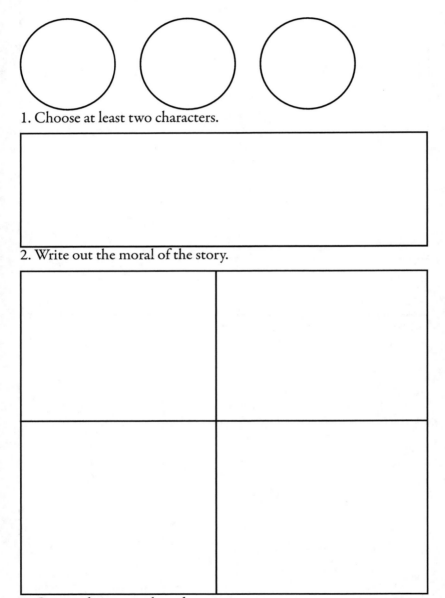

1. Choose at least two characters.

2. Write out the moral of the story.

3. Create a basic storyboard.

4. Write the fable!

# FABLE BUILDER

# FINAL WORD

My first journal was a twenty-page, wide-ruled notebook that had been stapled together on one side. This primitive binding was the preferred method for early elementary school teachers and, at the time, it made the book look like an elaborate homework assignment. I remember this green construction-paper-covered journal as my first true possession. It would take ages to fill that little book with sentences about my family, our car, my favorite color, and things that I saw outside my window.

The family house sat on a small hill on an acre of land with a hundred pine trees protecting it from the noise of the road. My mother's father had planted those pine trees and, throughout my youth, my brother and I would create worlds under their branches. In the winter, we rode sleds so fast they broke the sound barrier. In the summer, we climbed high in the trees and plotted secret missions for treasure hungry adventurers. On that acre of land, we trained as international spies and swung across the wildest woods with Tarzan. James Watson told us about the mysteries he helped solve with his incredible partner, Sherlock. R.L. Stein babysat for us on rainy days. We learned to be reporters from TinTin and expected our pets to be as tenacious as the little dog, Snowy.

The stories we heard as children echoed for years, and my brother and I still tell versions of them today. I moved out of that house a long time ago. I took a job out of state. Now, I live in Edgewater, just a block away from the Western shore of Lake Michigan.

I am writing this in December, but it still feels like late fall. There is no snow on the ground and the shortest day of the year has already passed. On days like this, when it is still too cold to be outside, I sit in my office and type. I try to conjure up stories from when I was young. I like to explore well known characters that were born long before my time. Sometimes, I pick up random pieces of inspiration from a book. I write lines based on other things that I have read. I admire archetypes and use them in short fiction.

This book will serve as your inspiration from the best of Aesop's Fables. Write stories based on the characters that were mentioned inside. Their brief descriptions act as rough skeletons. Fables are timeless.

I hope you find as much to admire in these fables as I do.

I hope you can create something new with them.

When you get stuck, read a fable.

# INDEX

# INDEX